Casablanca:
the Poem

Casablanca:
The Poem

from the award-winning motion picture starring
Humphrey Bogart, Ingrid Bergman, & Paul Henreid

Kildare Dobbs

Ekstasis Editions

Canadian Cataloguing in Publication Data

Kildare Dobbs
Casablanca: the poem

ISBN 1-896860-58-3

1. Casablanca (Motion Picture)—Poetry. I. Title.
PS8507.O35C37 1999   C811'.54   C99-911052-7
PR9199.3.D525C37   1999

Published in 1999 by:
Ekstasis Editions Canada Ltd.   Ekstasis Editions
Box 8474, Main Postal Outlet   Box 571
Victoria, B.C. V8W 3S1   Banff, Alberta ToL oCo

THE CANADA COUNCIL LE CONSEIL DES ARTS
FOR THE ARTS   DU CANADA
SINCE 1957   DEPUIS 1957

Casablanca: The Poem has been published with the assistance of a grant from
the Canada Council and the Cultural Services Branch of British Columbia.

For Linda

CASABLANCA:
CREDITS

Richard (Rick) Blaine	Humphrey Bogart
Ilsa Lund	Ingrid Bergman
Victor Laszlo	Paul Henreid
Captain Louis Renault	Claude Rains
Major Heinrich Strasser	Conrad Veidt
Signor Ferarri	Sydney Greenstreet
Ugarte	Peter Lorre
Carl	S.Z.Sakall
Yvonne	Madeleine LeBeau
Sam	Dooley Wilson
Annina Branel	Joy Page
Berger	John Qualen
Sacha	Leonid Kinskey
Pickpocket	Curt Bois
Jan Brandel	Helmut Dantine
Singer	Corinna Mura

A Hal B.Wallis Production
Directed by Michael Curtiz
Screenplay by Julius J. and Philip Epstein, Howard Koch
From a play by Murray Burnett and Joan Alison
Director of Photography Arthur Edison A.S.C.
Music by Max Steiner
Art Director Carl Jules Weyl

A Warner Bros — First National Picture

CONTENTS

Introduction

The film *Casablanca* was a product of Hollywood's studio system, one of some 50 pictures produced by Warner Brothers in 1942. It was the work of many hands in a system where the producer was the master and the director the man who called the shots. (The director, as Gore Vidal remarked, overstating it, was the son-in-law.) The controlling genius of *Casablanca* was the producer, Hal B. Wallis, as Aljean Harmetz documents in the definitive record of the making of the motion picture in *Round Up the Usual Suspects*, so that it was not quite the happy accident of popular legend. But whatever its provenance *Casablanca* is a work of art resonant with ambiguity. It has persisted over 50 years as a myth of our time. A carefully restored print is available in video, which Warner Bros issued to celebrate the company's 75th anniversary in 1998.

The poem is a sequence inspired by the film, developing themes from the drama and meditating on the characters and historical setting. In a sense it is an experiment towards a more public poetry, using a well-known story as an organizing myth for a kind of cantata of verses — lyric, narrative and soliloquy.

The premise of the story is that two German couriers, carrying letters authorizing the bearers to pass frontiers without hindrance, have been murdered and the documents stolen. These passes bear the signature of General Weygand, the Vichy French commander. In the real world no such letters could have existed.

The action of the movie hurries us by the implausibility. And in any event it is clear that the story is imaginary. The Casablanca of the story is in the desert; in reality the city is in a wide fertile area. The fugitive resistance leader is a shining figure in white, accompanied by a radiantly beautiful woman. Again, the implausibility does not bother us. It all takes place in "a dream of the race," to use Jung's definition of myth. The many unlikely events in the story distract us no more than they would in a private dream. The realities of the dream exist in the golden world of imagination.

And as for deriving a poem from a film, why not? Motion pictures routinely take their matter from novels, plays, biographies. It's only fair that the tables should be turned.

Note on prosody. The metre throughout is syllabic, eleven to a line. Some poems are in Sapphic strophes, with three lines of eleven syllables followed by a fourth with five syllables.

One poem is an adaptation of the Renaissance *glosa*, used in Canada by P.K.Page. Here it is an invention evolved from lines of dialogue in the film.

PRELUDE

Entranced in the darkening picture palace,
as the music swells while the curtain dissolves
and the famous shadows appear on the screen
                                    to perform the myth,

the new lovers hold hands in their private cave
as chocolate soothes the opening sequence
and the lonely heart beats with inward thunder,
                                    sensing the neighbour;

and the voices and faces on the screen are
more real than our own, models for our small lives.
Some movie-buffs actually fall in love
                                    with the lovely wraiths

as once men loved mermaids and pursued them down
through green waters to the dark of the abyss
and quickly drowned, so now the quest is lethal,
                                    death to the spirit.

The screen is there to mark the frontier of dream:
we, here in our seats — the plebs chewing popcorn,
the elect making clever phrases — on this side;
                                    on that, fantasy.

In Casablanca, there lies the imagined scene,
world war, Nazis, refugees, black market and
a marvellously beautiful heroine.
                          Begin it, Sam. Play.

Play it, Sam.

Play it, Sam, as always it plays in our hearts,
and again a kiss, a sigh, O world, O time,
touch of ebony fingers, soft chords, black note
on keys of ivory, and ivory dice,
the wheel of chance spins, O love, *rien ne va plus!*

Play it again, Sam, is what we always say,
misquoting, happy as the night is long, and song
the ark that floats us on an ocean of dream,
the rhythm of voices, ocean surf surging on,
heard in our blood in this limbo by the sea

yet unseen, since the agonists perform indoors —
those who came for the waters were misinformed —
where lies and deception in a noble cause
move in slow foxtrot with love and faithlessness
possessed by music and the pain of lost love.

For we too have known that place away from place
that *boite de nuit* in the noisome dark kasbah
where lovers and enemies meet to parlay
and deal their cards with inscrutable faces,
some to be aced in spades, others to go free.

And we too have known that time away from time
as time goes by while the soft music plays on
even when all the musicians have gone home
and time goes by bye-and-bye when lovers meet
in the shadows to renounce true love and faith.

SMOKE AND *MERDE*

"A lot of cigarette smoke, a lot of *merde* "
was how it started, the writers' first idea,
so the men smoke, each in his own party style.
Rick does it skilfully, no smoke in his eyes,
the thing sticks to his lips, smoke all around him
like clouds on Olympus, and as for the Prefect,
when he's off duty he hides in his smokescreen.

The Gestapo are all sinister smokers,
narrowing eyes, the glowing cigarette-end
often a crude instrument of persuasion —
which may explain why Strasser smokes as he walks,
something not seen in more elegant units.
Obviously it hasn't done his teeth any good.

Ladies don't do it in public, or standing,
but may do it sitting, though never in bed —
should the Hayes office allow us to see that,
the post-orgasmic fix not yet acknowledged.
No one thinks of cancer or emphysema.

As for *merde*, it takes the form of epigrams
and urbane foreigners' wit, singing in bars,
drinking cointreau, cognac and the best champagne,
eating caviar from the tin with a teaspoon,
playing roulette, wearing white uniforms,
and plenty of exotic decorations,

but always enveloped and wreathed with grey smoke,
the cigarette-smoke which thickens with the plot,
until at last it spills outdoors as light fog,
into which the heroes stroll and then vanish.
It is the notorious fog of battle,
and maybe the mists of history as well.

SILENCES

What was left out to let the story appear?
A minaret first, somebody moving there;
the muezzin calls out the divine equation,
the high, unanswerable tautology:
Only God is God, e equals mc squared.
But this is not heard, Islam is silent here.
Often the story is in the silences.

The British come nearer after each reverse,
the glamorous Eighth Army, the splendid First,
wearing down Rommel and his Afrika Korps.
Why are they not heard from, and why not Islam?
Maybe because in this American dream
there can be no ancestors or near cousins,
and no God where there is drinking and smoking,
only democracy and its enemies.

SAM THE PIANO PLAYER

Ilsa asks who's the boy playing the piano
though he's wearing long pants and shaves every day,
a paid performer in a classy gin-joint.

It's been a long time, Sam, since the good old days.
That radiant smile alarms the piano player.
Yes ma'am, a lot of water under the bridge.

Such women, he knows, are nothing but trouble,
and who should know better than a poor black man
with the plantation blues in his finger ends,

who played downstairs in backstreet cat-houses
to the jangle of rusty bedsprings upstairs,
and the hardluck stories of teenage hookers.

Mister, the stories began, *I met a man* —
Rick heard these recitations often enough
but without the harmonics native to Sam.

Ladies and jellyrolls, listen to my songs,
my midnight flashbacks to the middle passage,
my black voice smoky with cannabis longings.

THE FALL OF FRANCE

Hear the words of the Calvinist André Gide
(dread of freedom was his strangest passion):
O incurably frivolous people of France!
                              (these his very words)

Yes, long before the war France stank of defeat —
Too much liberty has led to our downfall.
I do not love man, I love what devours him.
                              (this from Prometheus)

Nothing great is achieved but by sacrifice —
your dream is great, Hitler, but if it should fail,
what's left but death and utter devastation?
                              (and look, it did fail.)

AS TIME GOES BY

And as time goes by nothing changes or ages,
champagne is always Veuve Clicquot 'twenty-six,
Ilsa forever chaste as a Grecian urn,
forever frail and innocently faithless,
Rick's rictus a changeless mask of sacrifice,
Lou still only a poor corrupt official,
Vic forever the patriotic cuckold.

As time goes by white tuxedos and tunics
are still immaculate, the cause unsullied,
the Germans still barbarous in act and speech,
the French ever craven yet nobly spoken —
and we love Paris in the rain though seedy,
city of light in Ilsa's Nordic radiance
and Richard's loving, Here's looking at you kid!

And forever we look at her, the lovely Swede,
forever young and always in the best light,
shy in happiness, in tears noble, shining
in darkened rooms, the promise of her body
understated if at all expressed, her honour
chivalrously asserted by her lover,
as chivalrously accepted by her spouse.

We may wonder about that as time goes by,
how the young beauty gets to win two lovers
without blame, one French and one American.
America, the longed-for destination
of peace — and freedom-seeking Europeans —
as if there were no handguns in Manhattan.
French means unreliable, prating of *gloire*,
and expert in bed, if you can believe it.

Not to forget the young bride who comes to Rick
wanting to know if doing something naughty
for a good cause (i.e. an exit visa)
is all that bad. Having it off with Renault
is what she means, dear little vulgar Bulgar —
might be fun too if she could forget the shame.
But Rick, puritan in heart, saves her honour.

GONIF

Vultures, vultures, full of vultures! Watch yourself!
Watch yourself! warns the thief working the cafés,
mouth full of lusciously liquid els, his hand
in the pocket of a fellow refugee.
The gonif known, why is he tolerated?
Is he working for Renault or Ferrari,
or even Rick? or is he a metaphor
for the prevailing hypocrisy and crime?

Amusing little fellow! says the tourist
until, too late, he finds his wallet missing.
The thief, lost in the crowd, moves like quicksilver
through gaps in the plot, good for a laugh or two.

UGARTE

Trapped within the persona of Peter Lorre,
Ugarte cannot win trust or sympathy.
The squat figure and fawning mien summon up
                all of Lorre's past roles,

child murderer, pervert, soul lost in despair.
You despise me, don't you? he insists to Rick,
yet he has the dignity of a killer
                who's about to die.

I stick my neck out for nobody, says Rick,
shrugging off Ugarte's desperate appeal.
No one wastes a single tear on the trapped toad
                when his life's snuffed out.

Yet he was one of those who saved fugitives
with exit visas, passports, transit papers —
For a price, Ugarte, for a price! sneers Rick,
                who has saved no one.

His the righteous tone of one who stands aloof.
Sure, Ugarte was beyond help, the police
Would have caught and killed him wherever he hid,
                yet Rick had connived.

After Ugarte's arrest, this much is clear,
to save Rick's honour calls for some cleansing act
of violence, say, a Nazi sacrifice —
                            it will come to that.

Yes, he'll come to that in time, girded to act
as a warrior for the good cause. A soldier
kills without compunction when necessary.
                            Rick will be ready.

Though now he is confused, and will be more so
when love and self-pity mist up his vision
and the right path is hidden from his mind's eye,
                            his moment will come.

Like Arjuna, when Krishna, his charioteer,
rebuked his unmanly qualms at taking life,
Rick will return to his fore-chosen duty
                            in killing Strasser.

DIAMONDS

Diamonds are a drug on the market... We hear
the gutteral chaffer. A buyer's market,
for the sellers need money to stay alive,
to escape those advancing Nazi murderers,
buy food and medicine, pay bribes and airfares.
Now they're defenceless, vultures devour their life.

Diamonds are forever? Nothing lasts so long,
buy for a sultan's ransom, sell for a song.
Flashing blue malice, the diamonds bring bad luck
to their owners, dug up from blue clay and muck
and paid for in blood or long years in a jail cell.
These stones are coals from the furnaces of hell.

RICHARD/RICK

A man who looks like Bogie, grimace of pain,
the skull showing its contours under the skin,
fine hands and easy bearing, a clear presence
                                  in white tuxedo,

and quite the gentleman, though known to police.
I stick my neck out for nobody, he lisps,
and you wonder what brought him to this dead-end
                                  in Casablanca,

haven for fugitives from dictators' rage,
for the lucky, an airport departure lounge.
Rick's café here won't be his last address, on
                                  that you can rely

A man like that will put his life on hold
because of some terrible disillusion,
scowl as he smokes the cigarettes of despair,
                                  not drinking with guests.

There were betrayals no doubt, in childhood first,
perhaps by his mother, though he's not saying —
the rule is no questions in love as in war,
                                  and keep your head down.

Admitted: in Spain with the Loyalist troops
he looks on unblinking at blood and slashed throats
as his comrades knife landlords and priests, rape nuns
                                    all in the good cause.

Soldier, a grandmother moans, no one can win,
but this is certain, the poor lose all the wars.
Never say it's for us you fight — it's not true,
                                    you're murderers all.

Leave her, the commissar says, and take this whore
out of town to the hills, and then the bullet
in the back of the neck when she's looking away —
                                    this from a good guy.

Takes the girl to the hills as instructed, lights
her last smoke, asks her name, Concepción, she says
Spare me small talk, get it over, just do it!
                                    He's as pale as she.

Concepción, your name makes me nervous, he says.
Let's get the hell away, I'm through with this war.
Don't expect a thank you, is all she can say,
                                    and so to the woods!

Tough, in her teens, a juvenile delinquent,
the gypsy girl says, So I owe you my life.
Take then this body of the resurrection

                              as my sacrifice.

And later she says, I have an illusion,
an illusion for you, a sweet pain called love,
without it no two could ever stay as one,

                              as I will with you.

Later in Paris, during the *drôle de guère,*
he dreams of Concepción, killed right beside him
by a Fascist grenade, and wakes up in tears.

                              He takes to bourbon.

What's your nationality? Strasser will ask.
I'm a drunkard! Rick will growl (by then untrue).
Born in New York, if that will help you any.

                              And cannot go home.

And it seems that destiny is taking a hand,
(in Rick's phrase) when he meets the lovely Ilsa,
and they love each other at once, forever,

                              all over again.

A FIGHT FOR LOVE AND GLORY

Victor's the noble one, but what's he about,
does he not seem rather a chinless wonder?
Impassive as a tombstone, said to be Czech
but passing for French, as I happen to know.
I was there, in Casablanca at Rick's place,
when Victor entered (and so, of course, were you).
He stood up as a soldier for France and *la gloire*,
leading the Marseillaise, that song of empire,
not as a Czech, not against the butchery
of Lidice, or the murdering machine
that gassed Europe's Jews, gypsies and dissidents.
Nationalism, the French kind, was his fervour,
in this he was no different from Pétain.

PÉTAIN

Look at the big poster of Marshal Pétain:
Je tiens mes promesses, même celles des autres,
a Free French fugitive shot dead by police
in front of it. Here is the cross of Lorraine,
a question of legitimacy. Pétain
defeated, has pledged his word to lay down arms;
de Gaulle has no authority to break it.

So in effect he declares, *La France, c'est moi!*
His name supports it, yet he is a rebel,
guilty of high treason in the view of some.

Yet in the long view — such views as de Gaulle takes —
the generals of Vichy dishonoured France,
yes, Pétain is putain, de Gaulle upholds the right,
the honour of *La France* is saved by exiles
and by the communist underground at home.

Dance, Jellyroll, dance and be history's fool!
Jellyroll Putain, meet Jellyroll de Ghoul.
Your face on a poster's the wrong kind of fame,
keeping faith with Hitler's a loser's game.
Watch de Ghoul who right now don't got no respect —
after the war he's the one France will elect.

REFUGEES WAIT... AND WAIT...

Refugees wait. Prisoners know this distress
locked in their cells, killing time when all the time
time is killing them. Waiting for the last bus,
Ahmed suffers; at the hospital the wife
waits for the doctor. Patience means suffering,
and Islam is resignation to God's will.
Muslims have learned the soldier's art of blankness,
squatting in corridors, staring into air.
Doctor, dentist, lawyer, public officials
make you wait, and thus express the clear message:
Our time is precious, yours is of no account.

Real Casablanca is a modern city,
in cities time is owned by the management,
here time is profit, time is money, punch the clock,
and charge for overtime at time and a half.
In farmland time is the sky, the sun and rain,
with seasons for planting, harrowing, ploughing,
and the sun's best days the happy harvest home.
At sea, the moon owns time, governing the tides,
the winds, the hurricanes, lightnings, neaps and springs,
until noonday, when the sun's height is taken,
and sailors know their place by the sun's zenith.
In the great sands and hammad of the desert
the sun for men, for women and beasts the moon,
measure the days, and set the five calls to prayer.

What we see are ghosts, see-through wraiths without breath,
repeating their agony through endless ages
never changing a syllable or a glance.
Time is the ironist that mocks our wishes,
now granting them too late. now disappointing,
as we run on and time runs on within us
like the tide that runs under the moving keel.
As time goes by, we go by, we go with it.

On the southern defiles of the High Atlas
where a rough road swerves along precipices
that fall far down to the tawny Sahara
by red walls of Ouarzazarte and beyond
there are points above dizzying gulfs and deep chasms
where you look over reaches of empty air
to a valley far off, far down, enclosing
floors of living green — the Prophet's own colour —
tiny date-palms shrunken by distance yet still
exquisitely drawn, each frond sharply distinct,
though the eye faints traversing that immense space,
and there, and there, the flash of mountain water
where the river Draa flows past sunburnt kasbahs
toward Zagora, M'Hamid, and then the sands,
the silent hammads and great dunes on the move.
Tombouctou, cinquante-deux jours by fast camel.

The Draa sighs in its wadi for distant seas,
longing to join in the everlasting deeps
of the great oceans. But the river shrinks from
ferocious suns; the river runs forever
and time goes by, by the parching sands engulfed,
and as time and river run, desire runs dry,
faint longings for the main deep at last shrivel
or dive under earth far from the Atlantic.
And like a letter long unanswered, burn out
the dying hope that once was green and fruitful,

Again, in Greenwich the dead empire sets time,
teaching the world's shipping and dockyard clocks.
The maestro beats it, the musicians keep it,
sad idlers on street-corners are wasting it.
In the film itself there is no time at all,
or rather a time that circles in a loop
and in which the images live forever
although by now the actors are all deceased,
their lines long since forgotten as life ebbs out.
There's still before and after an ever-*now*
and still time goes by, and never goes bye-bye
while you can run the videotape again.

Executive Summary

So play it again, Sam, as musical chairs,
stand up and change partners in threesomes and pairs;
couples and triangles complicate the tale —
whoever's left standing takes the lonesome trail.
Sam's jealous of Ilsa, he loves only Rick
Richard loves Ilsa so he's jealous of Vic,
Yvonne loves Rick while the barkeep loves her,
she boozes with Nazis, which makes quite a stir,
Victor loves Ilsa but *La France* even more,
though Ilsa loves Richard and France proves a whore.
Rick and Louis are left by themselves at the end,
and each to the other's a beautiful friend.
When shove comes to push — or the other way round,
no friend like a male friend can ever be found,
So into the fog march the cynical chums
to join the Free French to the rattle of drums.

Dumb academicals

There are other pairs, though not coupled in sex:
two cops, German and French, enemy and friend;
two in trade, Rick and the Fez, but which of them
is honest is by no means clear at first sight;
two fatties, Carl and the Fez, maybe both good;
Rick and Vic, though rivals, are two knights in white,
each with his demonic other in Strasser;
two men named for cars. Ferrari and Renault;
Rick and Louis, two cynics with hearts of fudge.

Victor and Strasser make another twosome,
as white to white they more or less represent
two rigid opinions in conflict, each one
mistaken from science of an earlier age.

It has to be said that the conflict is not
put in quite that way, being represented
in more or less sporting terms with money bets
as world-bully pitted against underdog,
a contest in which you can wager your heart.

Such pairings, though, may be less significant
than the shadowy lineaments of the myth
projected for us as the story goes on.
In shining white, Victor's the chaste Galahad,
who wins his lady by being cuckolded
by Launcelot (that's Rick), the demon-slayer
who sacrifices love for the duration.
Say, Ilsa while she lived was a good lover,
and therefore it may be she had a good end.

ECHOES –– *A GLOSA*

Play it, Sam, play 'As Time Goes By', sing it, Sam —,
Waters. What waters? We're in the desert here —,
I'm the only Cause I'm interested in —
It seems that destiny has taken a hand....

In the open sports car with wild hair blowing free,
the wind a tumult of caressing music,
or in the safehouse of a hotel bedroom,
the lovers sip champagne, embracing as they
discover love's customary ecstasy,
this now their final truth, and all others sham
or merely prelude to the sublime event.
Love is illusion, as the gypsy girl said,
without illusion there is no me and thee.
Love's insubstantial as a cabaret tune --
the piano-player knows what she wants, Yes ma'am.
Play it, Sam; play 'As Time Goes By', sing it, Sam.

He sings into memory the sad sweet song
that bears with its melody the mythic town,
in a desert that is in truth Hollywood.
On maps it is a port on African shores
crowded with fugitives from the Gestapo,
the halfway house of isolationist fear.
Who sings the song? an American negro.
himself a servant in this French colony
whose people bear no part in any action,
invisibles whose moment has not yet come—
the waters of Babylon are everywhere.
Waters? What waters? We're in the desert here.

43

You must remember this, it was about love
and faithlessness, and finding the way at last
in a world of murderous angers and greed.
A man who can bear the cruelties of war
but not desertion by a woman he loves
finds a corrupt city where he can begin
again. Seeking the waters of redemption
he finds the balm of arid neutrality,
dry consolations of money, cold embrace —
a kiss is just a kiss, a sigh just a sigh.
Where he comes from, self-interest is no sin:
I'm the only Cause I'm interested in.

It's still the same old story, no one's immune,
the world comes to us no matter where we hide,
look away, it's there whether you see or not.
Proverbial wisdom says love will find a way;
but this we do know, that it's always too late
when the message in the bottle floats to land.
And when love returns it's never quite the same,
each wound leaves us weaker, more apt to evade
choice, as frailty becomes the wisdom of age.
No longer strong enough for the sweet madness
that seized our hearts before we could understand.
It seems that destiny has taken a hand.

Rick in Abyssinia

A man called Rimbaud ran guns here before me,
antique muskets for Menelik, king of kings,
lion of Judah, heir to great Solomon
                              a long time ago

wrecked and ruined by bad debts and hostile tribes
and by a tumour which cost his leg and life
with bad treatment in, I think it was Aden
                              but he died in France.

I heard he was a poet who gave up art
and with it lost hope and love, to go among
people whose lives he did not care to enter.
                              I'm kind of like him.

Like him I lost my way, feeling death in me
and failure of all aptness for happiness.
Only in danger could I feel half alive —
                              I lived on my luck.

Like him I ran old arms and ammunition
and dealt with the tribesmen, who were honest enough.
Fascist spies noticed my caravan, and put
                              a price on my head.

Hiding with the Danakil, I was almost
caught by patrolling Bersaglieri, but stood
and fought them off, killing a few. The tribesmen
                              massacred the rest.

I got away in the end, and was well paid.
Not that I cared. The desert entered my mind,
wild as the men and animals who lived there,
                              raging for freedom.

The fundamental things

Shores of Africa, an ocean warm as blood,
the harbour built by white men in nineteen eight.
A night wind blows, scattering hiccuping speech
of hooded forms, shrouded in jellabias,
Arab and Negro, Berber and Tuareg.
Dark rocks oppose the surf where, not far offshore
rise shadowy walls of a Moorish saint's tomb;
and over roofs and minarets the lighthouse
sends its glare. Casablanca was from the first
a place of death, eight construction workers slain
before the new harbour mole was in its place,
and that brought in the French with logic and guns.

Rick says, I'm going to die in Casablanca,
it's a good spot for it.
                    A good spot for it,
the new city is a commercial centre
of French enterprise around the medina.
Labyrinth of medieval trades and smells,
the spice-vendors' mounds of yellow turmeric,
red paprika, saffron and henna, rosebuds,
coriander, cloves from Zanzibar, cumin,
pickled lemons, tubs of herbed butter, bay leaves.
Sunlight striped by matting awnings, and in here
a bathhouse selling steam, hot water, massage,
broken tiles, grease, old skinny men in loincloths.
Then hills of fruit, gold oranges, apricots,
quinces, pomegranates, dates and nectarines,
and the rug-sellers, and the embroiderers,
and the French wives and mistresses out shopping.

THE PREFECT OF POLICE.

I joined them later, raw from filthy trenches,
my heart a no-man's-land where youth lay bleeding,
still racked with victory and its disillusion.
To expect the worst, that was the safe policy,
make friends of the friends of death, the dark princes
of the High Atlas kasbahs, in whose dungeons,
lightless and airless, without food or water,
our enemies and theirs died their dreadful deaths.

As for myself, I did what I had to do,
whatever it took, until in time I rose
to a rank that allowed me to delegate.
Others did my dirty work, I had the fun.
Women were always my pastime. I love them.
When I was young I went for the warm matrons.
learning from them what they were glad to teach me,
grateful for my heat as I for their technique.
Often they were wives of brother officers,
men who had come to Africa for the boys,
deserters from their duties on the home front.

My loves grew younger as myself became older,
bored by my aging skill — why did I always
tell the same lies? Why did they always believe?
True Love struck just once, with pains worse than toothache,
ecstasy of sorrow and exaltation.
I invented the visa difficulty
to bring me bedmates of briefest duration.

Something went sour for me when the Germans came,
my own face in the glass was what I saw for,
though cruel, they were no more so than ourselves,
though more methodical, driven by doctrine —
they put the boots to Europe, we to Africa.
In duelling chorus, *Die Wacht am Rein* sounds
in harmony with our own *La Marseillaise*,
no discord there, though sung in competition.
One might think Strasser a more suitable friend
for a colonial flic than a drifter from
America with disappointed ideals,
broken heart and monumental self-pity.
The Bosch is after all an old acquaintance,
familiar from earlier wars and conflicts,
a coarser alter ego fired up with cant —
with Kant and Hegel and the odious Wagner —
and that's the distinction that sets us apart.
Me, I've no convictions, I blow with the wind —
just now the wind happens to be from Vichy,
but any moment soon it will be changing.
A wild Nor'Wester threatens, a hurricane,
and Rick, my American friend's a portent,
a storm bird presaging the vast disturbance.

Meanwhile I wait from hour to ominous hour,
postponing choice. Strasser and I are Europe
linked in the dance of ancient dialectic,
the Yank a persistent misunderstander,
an angry child of questionable parents,
believing himself the world's sole innocent.
But the Bosch lacks charm and the Yank makes me laugh.

A man who sees things has to be frivolous,
I have to make fun of my predicament.
I alone know where the bodies are buried,
a secret that's beginning to fester.
And yet it is not conscience that gives me pain
but the ugliness and the loss of honour.

Rick Returns

Noble of me, you think, to send her away —
think again, think how badly she used me,
sending her away was the purest revenge.
It's a sin to tell a lie, says an old song.
Listen, no woman will get that chance again!
But O the pity, so beautiful —yeah but
who cares? back home blondes are a dime a dozen.
Good luck to her with her sanctimonious spouse!
Sick of him already, but doesn't know it.
One of these days she'll run off with a waiter,
someone like my crazy Russian, and be rid
of highflown talk and high-minded posturing —
she knows that in power he'd be high-handed too.
I'll settle for the trenches again with Lou.

RENAULT'S KÉPI

Why do you keep me tilted to the right side?
Surely well-bred officers keep a straight cap.

When you appear and are instantly obeyed
it is because of my golden dignity.

Your own figure carries no air of command,
and to wear me awry just looks frivolous.

It's true Lord Beatty wore his cap on one side
because of a head-wound that ached on pressure.

That was excusable, brought no disrespect,
but it is otherwise when the lapse is willed.

Solomon's crown slipped down over his right eye
because he'd lost compassion for those he judged.

I wear your gold lace "at a jaunty angle,"
the way actors do, to impress young women.

The *képi* replies, King Solomon listened
when his crooked crown told him the nasty truth,

and the king of kings knelt down in gratitude,
and kept a straight crown from that day to his end.

YOU MUST REMEMBER THIS

We'll always have Paris, young lovers believe
who have strolled hand-in-hand in the Tuileries,

or boarded a *bâteau mouche* just for the ride
and stared for long hours into each other's eyes;

or who popped champagne corks in curtained bedrooms,
talking lazily through sexy afternoons,

or wandered under the plane trees by the quays,
browsing in the print-stalls on summery days;

but memory can be forgetful, soon, all too soon
Paris will fade, as beauty loses its soft bloom.

We'll always have Paris, old lovers declare,
sipping coffee and *fine* in the rain-washed air,

but who was with me then, I almost forget,
except that she was lovely, and good in bed,

and that the Germans wore grey and she wore blue
and then there was Sam, who used to play our tune.

Whatever became of him I'd like to know;
he seemed like a fellow with places to go.

Now what was her name? the girl who told me lies,
not that it matters at all as time goes by.

GIDE AGAIN

One curious observation of the *savant*,
"We have everything to learn from Germany,"
and then, "she has everything to take from us."

                                               Mostly she took Jews.

Above all, France needs one maxim from Goethe:
"Untersuchen was ist, und nicht was behagt."
To grasp that would help France understand her fall

                                            and help her atone.

Among the things Germany took from the French
was awareness of their humiliation.
They hardly felt it, and could sing, *Le jour de*

                                            gloire est arrivé!

ILSA

Dark winters by the fjord, brief, burning summers,
after the first tender green of the beech leaves
and daffodils at the forest's shaded edge
and the romp round the Maypole at midsummer
and the king's yacht at moorings in the harbour:
my growing up in Oslo, then to Paris
for talking in cafés and at the Sorbonne,
conversing with architecture and statues,
humbled by Haussmann's prospects of masonry.
Playacting, perhaps, in intellectual games,
cigarettes, saxophones, existential *angst*
until the day when I heard shocking doctrine —
Victor with his reasoned certainties, his scorn
for the chatter of those idle afternoons.

As a hand on my thigh, a gentle caress,
were his noble abstractions. Revolution
took my heart, and this surrender I called love.
I am a Norsewoman; I led him to my bed.
My man, overwhelmed with honour, insisted
on marriage, in secret for my protection.

He was possessed by what he called the Struggle —
no, not arm-wrestling or street-fights, just meetings,
clandestine transmitters and printing presses.
Come the revolution, we'd declare ourselves,
but for now, the Struggle, the meetings, the words.
Never forget, these were words that could kill us.

In Prague arrested, he was taken away
to be put to the question, electric shock,
beatings, cigarette-burns, darkness, narrow cells —
unbearable to think what was done to him.
Now no more playacting, the Struggle was real.
Love sustained him, he said, as well as the Cause —
that was the iron hook that grappled my heart.

Escaping, he was gunned down and left for dead.
Once assured the rumour was certainly true,
I too died for a while, though still on my feet.
In nightmares I witnessed his choking on blood,
his weak cries for help, his shuddering last breath,
and night after night saw his image fading
until I felt only his words were still alive.

Then, O forgive me! I felt glad he was gone,
the burden of virtue was lifted at last,
and myself free to live in imperfection:
The truth is I was not so bad after all,
though not made for virtue — is any woman?
Virgins of Christ may wither away in cells,
forgetful of the parable of talents —
such rejections insult the divine giver.
We are not made for sacrifice but for love.
Not a walled garden bright with hidden flowers,
not a fountain sealed from all but the master,
but an open park where all desire may stroll,
look, breathe, admire, refresh the thankful spirit,
though none may break the branch or gather blossoms
without the lady's wish and loving consent.

I stared at the plane trees, the random patched bark,
freckled sunlight on pavement, the world was here
in the ruby light shining from my wine glass
and when I looked up it was into new eyes
through a blue mist of sunlit cigarette-smoke.

The man's eyes — "Here's looking at you. kid!" he said.
Therefore I danced and laughed and love opened me
as rosebuds open, thighs in languor loosened,
I breathed his male cedar and cigarette scents
and loved his voice even more than what he said
of parched lands of sun and colour, blood spilt
where my love lost youth and innocence in war's
horror and corruption, but found his heart's force.
Yet he was damaged, his trust a fragile thing,
and for his weakness no less I held him dear.

RICK AND CATULLUS

Furi et Aureli, comites Catulli
sive ad extremos penetrabit Indos...

The poet had two good friends and I have Sam
though I find my way to the far African
shore where the evening wave's long-sounding echoes
                                    tumble and thunder,

or buy old rifles from pederast Arabs
and run them into Ethiop savannas
for Danakils who fight like fiends to cut off
                                    Italian privates,

or though I travel to the edge of the world
and beyond to the deserts of ice and frost,
O dear friend who, despite the odds, is willing
                                    to brave all with me,

take this word to my girl: Let her not look back
to my love the way it was, for by her guilt
it's a fallen meadow-flower that has been bruised
                                    by the passing plough.

CARL

We did hear the waiter call him Professor,
his former title in the town of Salzburg
where he was weaned on *chocolate torte mit Schlag,*
musical composition his profession.
This good man did not accept Hitler's Anschluss
or cosy up to the Nazi *Schweinerei.*
He escaped while the Gestapo looked for him,
arriving in Casablanca with nothing.
Rick took him in, made him his major domo.
A clever manager and tireless worker
he serves in secret with the French resistance.

2.

Carl's the soft fat man as Ferrari's the hard,
all sentiment and fleshy solicitude,
almost the clown, yet for all his wobbling flesh
he's cool and courageous, shrewd in deception.

Here we see two aspects of excarnation,
not the word made flesh, but the flesh made word.

FERRARI

The man who looks like Greenstreet, called Ferrari,
is solid as a house, and keeps a servant
to clip his toenails, put on his socks and shoes.
Too fat to stoop, at least not to acts like that,
he does not deserve Rick's scorn. A businessman
dealing in the town's leading commodity,
namely, human lives, he does the best he can
to serve the needs of desperate customers,
and make a living. If doctors profit from
illness and pain, and lawyers from fraud and crime,
Ferrari profits from scarce necessities
and from the black market in new medicines.
Graceful in movement for all his bulk, he is
sensitive, polite and ready to be kind.
He gives free advice to Colonel McCormack
of *The Chicago Sun* as also to Rick,
and incidentally to America —
that isolationism is dumb politics.
Alarmed by his friend's rash hubris, he exclaims,
Don't be a fool, Rick!
                    But folly's Rick's function,
without fools there could be no story, no plot
and stiff pride will savage his heart in the end.
Ferrari is the bearer of surprises.
It is known to few that in his hat or fez
is coiled a catheter of indian rubber
with which he relieves himself at intervals,
not caring to hazard prostate surgery
in a town so famous for making eunuchs.

I was born here, to a Berber market girl
and a Spanish soldier or a Roman priest,
she was not sure which, but called me Ferrari
after a car she saw just before my birth.
I grew up Muslim. I believe devoutly
in the discipline of the free marketplace,
which in this time and place is called black market.
The Prophet, peace be unto him, was in trade,
which included traffic in black ivory,
that is, in Negro slaves, at that time, legal.
I myself make no slaves, I deal in free souls,
do what I can for them, and if I kill flies
it's because they bring typhoid and cholera.

THE BLUE PARROT

The Blue Parrot — blue is the sky, is the day —
for coffee and business at Ferrari's place
everything workaday as Rick's is for dreams.
No swindlers here, no confidence-men or cheats,
the coffee's Arabian, black and sweet and strong,
and what's your tipple, Scotch, cognac, rum, Bourbon,
or maybe you prefer Moroccan mint-tea —
the point is to keep a clear head for the deal.

The blue parrot is a creature of the air
yet talks like you and me. What he sees up there
can't be expressed, to ask is not our place.
As the churchyard Dane said of the Knight of Faith,
there's no hint in this house of the Absolute,
what you see is what you get, in its plain truth,
in its suchness and whatness, all's plainest prose.
It is all quite respectable, and duller
than criminal in its everyday colour,
and long before curfew-time the place is closed.

RICK

Renault's my friend, and still no better than I,
which ain't saying much — see my trick roulette wheel,
the mean way I treated Yvonne, who loved me,
my refusal to help refugees escape.
He's a flic in Casablanca, for a start —
which will make him an agent of the *Main Rouge,*
state terrorists who murder freedom fighters
Not so bad as the Gestapo, he protests.
At least we didn't bomb the soukhs Christmas Eve
like the Nationalists, he said, and by the way
I never killed for money, not even once.

Well, neither did I, but it is kind of sad
when a guy is reduced to such an excuse.
Now we leave playing at grownups and workers
to serve as carefree soldiers, jolly shirkers.

Carry a broom all day, never volunteer
and — as always my own personal motto —
never stick your neck out, not for nobody.
Pursue the soldier's joys: hot meals, dry bedding,
poontang where you can find it without wedding.

STRASSER

Officious functionaries, cruel schoolmarms,
lowlife tyrants at frontiers and parking lots,
tax auditors, appointments secretaries,
jailers, union shop-stewards, bank managers,
city editors, passed-over careerists,
football coaches, masters-at-arms, drill sergeants,
plus of course brute policemen behind closed doors,
all these to the nth power is Major Strasser.

Learned his trade in Kaiser Willhelm's leaden days,
rooting like a boar in citizens' affairs —
most have something to hide, perhaps everyone —
and though hurt on active service by a bus,
never risked life or honour in the trenches.
Jobless after the war, he joined a Freikorps,
happy once more in uniform and jackboots,
Nazi Himmler his patron and salvation.
The Party had no more loyal liege than he.

Kill Jews and misfits, beat up faggots, yes sir!
Resemblance of his name to that of Streicher,
the bestial Gauleiter, forwards his career.
Soon the good follower becomes a leader
who has to conspire in office politics.
The Reich favours a young punk or psychopath
over an experienced professional.
This Casablanca spiel is Strasser's last chance,
failure to checkmate Victor will destroy him,
yet his hands are tied by neutral protocol,
an 'incident' could be as bad as defeat.

Fear turns mere malice into lethal venom
and Strasser is never averse to killing
and unlike Renault will do the dirty himself,
not trusting mere sadists with this kind of work.
The code does not permit one to enjoy it,
a strict officer feels sorry for himself
should an unfortunate incident occur.

Victor

"Man is born free, and everywhere is in chains."
That much seems self-evident. We use all means

to overthrow the tyrants and their bullies
as a first step and, after that, we can seize

their power and profit to set up the domain
of reason and justice and the people's reign.

Our speech is the voice of History itself,
we shall not shirk the duty to speak out and tell

kings and dictators that their sun has gone down,
and we the people — that's the Party for now —

conceding each his need, from each will demand
the best that unselfish effort can command.

America, last, best hope of humankind,
we come to free you from capitalist swine!

Well, of course one can only put it that way
for use in quite elementary stages,

but the objective facts are more complicated.
For example, Ilsa's much more than my mate,

I need her, she embodies my ideal love
in certain ways the Party might not approve.

I'd see her saved before myself for good cause:
she knows too much and under torture might talk.

She sees me as an example and victim
of persecution and misunderstanding.

We may utilize such simplifications
in the pre-revolution situation.

They'll love my blonde wife in the United States
where you can win elections just with your face

and with your wife's face and other body parts
as well as by normal political arts.

Ilsa'll outdraw even Madame Chancre-Jack
with Luce and the China lobby at her back.

I'm aware that I myself seem somewhat cold,
but my wife's beauty turns everything to gold.

We need those papers to begin our escape,
Ilsa must procure them, whatever it takes.

If she has to give herself, no one objects.
Compared with the great Cause, how trivial is sex!

THE POET IN THE PICTURE

Summer nineteen-forty-two in Manhattan
on a run ashore from our old destroyer,
penniless yet proud of our bluejean collars,

my shipmates and I, we strangled a baron,
A Frenchman and probably a brown hatter
but he really was a Monsieur le Baron.

He bought us drinks in a bar on the west side.
He said, I'm desolate about my country —
and yet New York is so beautiful at night,

the skyscrapers like marble in the moonlight
and the lights blazing when Europe's lights are out —
and next thing you know, you tread on spat-out gum.

It was hot that summer, on street corners
steel counters were open to sell lime rickeys.
Men called, Wuddya say, sailor? Girls sang, Hi!
a pharmacist cried, Hey, hands across the sea!

In far off Hollywood *Casablanca* was
in production, to be released November
as Americans landed in Morocco.

Ourselves at sea in half a gale, escorting
a slow convoy of oil, food and munitions,
America now stirring in the enormous
commotion of world war. Beside that Titan
we felt small, being young, and expendable,
our strength not amounting to Rick's hill of beans.
If mother could see me now! a messmate laughs,
glad to be out of range of her rolling pin.

Around us the labouring ships, the commodore's
flickering with coded signals, the breaking seas.
Under our keels sea-monsters swam with U-boats;
between us and Davey Jones' locker the skin
of our hull, mortal danger too familiar
to notice, not knowing our destination,

ready for violence at a moment's notice
anytime anywhere. Cold and crudely victualled,
not enough sleep, red-eyed and wet through, we laughed
and skylarked around, dodging the bosun's mate,
or smoking in the heads, chipping off old paint
to paint more. War let us off the moral hook.

Towards Christmas that year as moviegoers wept
at the slow dance of Rick and Lou in midlife
and the sly moves of lovely Ilsa in love,
the western ocean took on a strange colour.
We left our convoy in heavy seas and turned
to stem a hurricane that savaged our ship.

Engulfed in howling night dazzled with lightning,
and seas like Himalayas of black water,
the ship was like to break her back and founder.

Bravely the good ship rode the crags and valleys,
sleepless the matloes toiled to keep her afloat
in mountainous seas that crashed on her slim waist
and carried away the boats and one smokestack,
and half the bridge and also, the Chief Stoker
whom no one loved, and probably he was pushed.

And all were speechless in the dreadful uproar
of wind and wild spray, and grimly thought the worst,
that all of us would drown in radio silence.
No one would know how we died — 'One of our ships
is missing' would be the signal, with 'Mayday,
Mayday' fading ever fainter on the air.

When suddenly all of us saw her, no one
knew how or why, Ingrid Bergman in a blaze
of St. Elmo's fire on top-hamper and shrouds!
Ours was a ghostly ship, a *Flying Dutchman*;
fretted with flame the mast showed a mandorla,
and at its centre Ingrid incandescent!

Some thought she was the Virgin, and blessed themselves
others denied the apparition or failed
to recognize her (a newcomer to us).
Still others feared the vision was sent from hell.
She faded then, black night rushed to swallow all,
but seas fell calm, alive we made our landfall.

So I, *laus deo* in London, surviving
in demob suit and cardboard shoes, a civilian,
went to the flicks and took in *Casablanca,*
and there she was again, the same Ingrid Bergman,
her lovely hair and teeth, that radiant scrubbed look,
Shining with promise of happiness, of life.
Pray for us, fair Ingrid, now and at our death:
pray for us, bright star, now and at our last breath.

LUCK

Luck is the dark enigma in love and war
and like God's grace cannot be earned or compelled.
The croupier dutifully fixing the odds
cries, *La partie continue! Marquons les jeux!*
and yet what's the use when the house always scores —
that's to say, he wins whose one Cause is himself,
and note, this is the Café Américain.

In this shrine of freedom and the bottom line,
les jeux sont faits! which of course means you can't win.
Look at it this way, honest Rick takes the cash
you need for your visa — and gives you zero.
Nought plus nought equals nothing, as you well know.

Take cash to Ferrari, though, he'll make your luck,
with visa, contraband, whatever you lack.
With the fat man, you get just what you pay for,
and at times, if he likes your face, even more.

TRANSFIGURATION

In the last scene Rick becomes Bogie again,
arrayed in the trenchcoat of sincerity,
the soft felt helmet of righteousness and truth.
Riding on a scowl and shoeshine, he proclaims
the high message of the knight of the mean streets.
The sheriff from out of town turns in his star —
order is restored, our side will win the war.

Where Bogie's going no woman can be seen,
what he must be, no female can be part of,
and the problems of three little people do
not amount in the end to a hill of beans
compared to the vast upheaval of warfare
at sea in two oceans, on land in the four
continents, the whole world torn by total war.

The doctrine's false, we think. If the sparrow's fall
is remarked on high, by so much more the pains
of humans weigh in an ultimate balance.
Each person's absolutely valued in all
especially the one who looks like Bogie
in trenchcoat and fedora, an errant knight,
wounded himself, whose true love is sacrifice.

Of course he does not believe a word of this,
knowing that his oblation was a phony,
knowing that Ilsa was right, that he was weak.
No matter now that a kiss is just a kiss,
he has become 'Bogie', a changeless image,
a cardboard cut-out, a figure of day-dreams,
the trenchcoat man who's never quite what he seems.

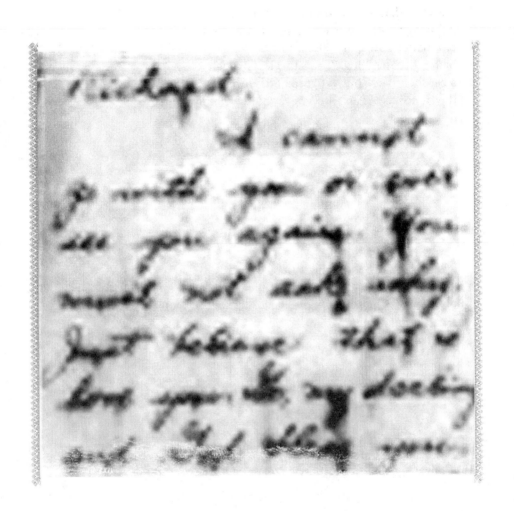

NIGHT

In this story, frame by frame, we observe,
most of the time that goes by is after dark.
Even here, many are afraid of the dark.
There was a prayer to lighten our darkness,
for once, a prayer answered, a wish come true
as flickering gaslight first, then electric
turned night to tungsten day, burning out terrors.
So Rick's Café Américain is a cave
of music and laughter, love and Lady Luck,
a festival of life against the vast night.

Though deeds of darkness still stain the curfew hours,
arrests, torturings and assassinations —
there's also the night flight to liberation,
as the lighthouse sends its beam over ocean.

High in the labyrinth of night the air-liner
speeds accurately to its destination,
cockpit aglow with dials, radio chatter,
cabin a softly-lit refuge from the dark.
In the metal belly some may doze awhile
but many are sleepless, beset by unspoken
doubts and apprehensions of what awaits them.
In the roar of engines voices seem to sound
in endless dispute, though the words are scrambled,
a cryptic muttering. Ilsa, bewildered,
stares at her husband, asleep in the next seat.
How can he sleep when her heart has been broken?
If only the gibbering voices would cease.

After all, this night flight is not her own choice:
leaving the thinking to her lover was wrong —
he passed her off to Victor like a parcel.
Staring at the window to her left, she tries
to look out into night, but sees her own face,
pale and shadowed, and hears the dark gibberish,
and next moment one voice is distinct, saying,
Resignation's not an act of moral choice.
How can he sleep when her conscience has spoken?
None of which signifies. The story's over.

THE END

You are still in the dark on this side of the screen
as the image fades, leaving the words THE END.
What was it you saw in the moving shadows?

Faces bigger than houses that loom and shine
with enormous meaning, Ilsa's mute question,
Rick's pain, Victor's impenetrable virtue,

the hurried speeches, everlasting goodbyes,
murmured blessings, tears beyond explanation,
angers choked down, defeat and triumph, the fog

of love and war, dark Africa, O music,
as the fatal spouses fly away to freedom
and the warlike bachelors stay to fight on,

light out for the territory like Huck Finn,
refusing domesticity, the old snare,
for the clean blade of a battle you can win.

A place you can smoke and drink all you want to
where the limits are clear since death draws the line —
was that the attraction? What was it to you?

Was it merely the clash of fierce opinions,
fascist and communist, or something less grand,
and yet of greater weight, the same old story,

love in the desert, cigarette smoke and merde,
as time went by, as time goes by once more?
The insufferably melodious refrain

breaking your broken heart all over again.
When the lights come up bright and the curtain falls,
you will remember this, and remember all.